# The Healing Crystals for Y Heart, Min

CW00481097

## Chakras, Energy, Mindfulness, Protection, Comfort & Peace

By

# Grace Whisenant

**Copyrighted Material**

*Copyright © 2020 – **Valley Of Joy Publishing Press***

All Rights Reserved.

*No part of this publication may be reproduced, stored in a retrieval system or transmitted in any form or by any means, electronic, mechanical, photocopying, recording or otherwise without the proper written consent of the copyright holder, except brief quotations used in a review.*

Published by:

**Valley Of Joy Publishing Press**

Cover & Interior designed

By

Jenny Coburn

*First Edition*

# Contents

Introduction ...........................................................7

Chapter 1: The History and Evolution of Crystal Healing 11

Crystals and Stones Around the Globe........................16

Egypt ...........................................................16

Greece..........................................................18

China ...........................................................19

India............................................................20

South America...............................................21

Scandanavia.................................................22

Crystals in Religion ...........................................24

The History of Crystal Healing ...........................26

Crystal Healing Today.......................................29

Alternative Holistic Medical Practices ...................31

Chapter 2: Exploring Chakras and Charts........................35

The Root Chakra..............................................37

The Sacral Chakra ...........................................38

The Solar Plexus Chakra ...................................38

The Heart Chakra............................................39

The Throat Chakra ...........................................40

The Third- Eye Chakra ......................................41

The Crown Chakra.................................................42

Balancing Your Chakras with Healing Crystals............43

The Root Chakra...............................................44

The Sacral Chakra.............................................44

The Solar Plexus Chakra....................................45

The Heart Chakra .............................................45

The Throat Chakra............................................45

The Third- Eye Chakra .....................................46

The Crown Chakra ...........................................46

How to Balance Your Chakras .................................46

Using Crystal Grids ..............................................48

Making a Crystal Grid .......................................50

Crystal Shapes and Structures .................................52

A Tumble Stone ................................................54

A Pyramid Crystal.............................................55

Crystal Spheres ................................................56

A Heart Crystal.................................................57

A Standing Point...............................................58

A Crystal Angel ................................................59

A Crystal Wand.................................................60

Chapter 3: Choosing Your Crystals............................62

Choosing a Crystal............................................................63

   Call onto the crystal that is best for you....................63

   Wait to have a physical reaction to a crystal.............64

   Experiment with different stones..............................65

   Using your astrological sign as a guide. ...................65

Choosing a Crystal with a Purpose .............................68

Chapter 4: Caring for Your Crystals & Other Uses..........113

The In's and Out's of Buying Crystals Online..............114

   Tip #1: Always buy from a well- known, reputable
vendor. ...................................................................116

   Tip #2: Use your own research to guide your way. .116

   Tip #3: Always, always check the price!....................117

   Tip #4: Be aware of the red flags and steer clear from
questionable merchants...............................................117

Caring for Your Crystals: Cleansing and Recharging..118

   Water Cleansing ......................................................119

   Nature Cleansing .....................................................120

   Sunlight & Moonlight Cleansing ............................120

   Sage or Sweetgrass Cleansing .................................121

   Sound Cleansing.......................................................121

   Recharging Crystals .................................................122

Safely Storing Crystals.................................................123

Other Ways to Use Crystal Healing ............................125

Tools ...............................................................125

Programming ................................................126

Other Ways to Use Your Crystals ...............................128

Wear your crystals. ......................................128

Put them in your pocket, purse, or backpack. .........128

Use your crystals in meditation. .............................128

Create a crystal layout on your body before starting
the day. ..........................................................129

Add them to your bath. ............................................129

Add them to your ritual. .............................................129

Precautions ...........................................................130

Chapter 5: The Other Side of Crystal Healing ................132

Conclusion ...................................................................139

# INTRODUCTION

N amaste! Welcome my friend, and thank you for accepting my invitation to explore the world of crystal healing.

I have been practicing crystal healing for well over a decade, and have worked tirelessly to create the very best book possible for you to guide you through this journey. I know that the decision to make this purchase doesn't come easy for everyone.

Introducing the concept of any new age practice is so against the conventional conditioning we've been brought up in, many approach the subject with a closed mind before ever truly giving it a chance. If you are one of those people, or even just someone who is a little nervous coming into this practice, I invite you now to open your mind.

Crystal therapy, although classified as "new age," is not new at all. In fact, it dates back thousands of years to ancient civilizations. The Sumerians, Egyptians, Mayans, and even Native Americans used crystals and gemstones for protection, healing, and transformation.

The practice can be found in nearly every culture, country, and religion around the world; deeply rooting itself into the way we live our lives today. What I am going to teach you in this book isn't fiction or information I made up based off of my own experiences. It's a tradition that has been passed down from generation to generation for centuries, leading up to this point right now when I pass it onto you.

This isn't a potions cookbook or some fictional children's fairy tale about flying brooms and moonlight rituals. Although, I do have to mention that the moon does make an appearance once or twice. This is a history lesson, a geology textbook, and instructional manual all in one complete package.

My goal for this book was to answer any questions you might have, spark your curiosity, and show you that healing yourself and others with crystals isn't as fanciful as it sounds.

Over the last few years, alternative wellness practices, like salt therapy lights and yoga classes have officially made their way into the mainstream. Crystal healing as a form of therapy and self-care has increasingly gained popularity, popping up all over social media, YouTube, yoga studios, and even on your coworker's desk. In fact, consumers in the United States spend approximately thirty billion dollars every year on alternative and holistic medicine.

Alternative medicine has only become taboo within the last hundred years or so. Before modern medicine, it was the way that we as a society lived and evolved. It is one of the reasons why we have progressed as far as we have.

What do you think happened when people got sick five hundred years ago? That they were just left alone to either fight the disease or die? Saying that holistic and new age medicine is all based on placebo effects or not backed by enough scientific evidence is to ignore our entire history as a race, save for the last hundred years.

My hope for this book is to shed a genuine, bright light on the practice of crystal healing. You are going to learn everything you need to speak intelligently about the practice, choose the crystals that are right for your intentions, understand how crystal healing works, and manipulate the natural energies radiating all around us to manifest your desires.

Now, as an author and well-meaning individual, I have the responsibility to remind you that this book is not a substitute for consulting a healthcare professional. The information that I share with you relating to medical and health conditions and treatments is for informational purposes.

I do encourage you to practice this healing method with an open mind, as I did when I began my own journey all those years ago. I am nothing, if not a survivor. I have experienced trauma, tragedy, loss, depression, and a medical diagnosis that was on track to end in the worst way.

In the face of all this adversity, I held strong to my beliefs, my faith. Knowing both sides of the coin, I understand that the naysayers do come from good intentions. As a practiced crystal healer, I also know what power lies in store for those who are willing to approach this practice with an open mind.

Now, close your eyes and take a deep breath. Allow your doubt and stress to melt away, clearing your attention to focus only on the material at hand. Beyond this page is the first step on your journey to self-discovery and healing far greater than what you've experienced before. And with this final word, I wish you the very best moving forward as we travel together.

# CHAPTER 1: THE HISTORY AND EVOLUTION OF CRYSTAL HEALING

For as long as humans have existed on this planet, we have shared an attraction and fondness for beautiful crystals and stones. If you explore our history over the last two thousand years and beyond, you will see that nearly every ancient culture utilized gemstones and crystals, believing in their power over the physical elements of this world. Crystals, minerals, and stones alike were used to release physical, mental, and especially spiritual blockages that inhibit our natural state of being and advancement; bringing us emotional and spiritual balance.

Over the last hundred years or so, holistic and alternative healing methods fell to the wayside as modern medicine took over. Even with natural and holistic practices making a comeback in the last ten years, many people will still give you weird looks if talk about alternative medicinal practices. Techniques such as crystal healing, reiki, and even homeopathy are seen as outdated, risky, and suggestive of a placebo effect rather than considered practical and valid methods of healing; regardless of their long and proven history throughout our lifetime as a species.

Although there is no way for us to know exactly when crystals were first used for something other than decoration, research and texts have proven that talismans and amulets were garnered and worn by the earliest civilizations. Many of the ornaments were even created organically. Beads carved from mammoth ivory have been found in Russian graves, and are believed to be more than sixty thousand years old. Researchers have also found beads crafted from shells and fossil shark teeth.

The use of precious stones can be found across continents and cultures. The Romans adorned healing stones as talismans and amulets to enhance health, protect them in battle, and show their status in society. The Ancient

Egyptians were known for burying their loved ones with quartz and other healing stones to safely guide their souls into the afterlife. The kings and queens of Egypt were decorated from head to toe in lapis lazuli and rubies to inspire enlightenment, stimulate their sex appeal, and awaken their third eye chakra. The belief in the power of crystals touched nearly every part of the world.

The fascination behind eye-catching stones and their power extended into ancient Chinese culture, especially in medicinal practices. For centuries, green jade has been valued as a lucky charm and magnet for prosperity. Ancient Grecians crushed hematite and rubbed the mineral all over their soldiers' bodies before battle to make them invincible. It's amazing how these precious stones and crystals have impacted nearly every culture; contributing to religion, mythology, scientific and medical advancement.

The methodical crafting of these gorgeous crystals has given us insight to the development of society as we know it today. The idea that thousands of years ago people believed gems and crystals held such value that they made them apart of daily life is truly intriguing. In fact, the oldest recorded amulet that was made of Baltic amber is estimated to be as old as thirty thousand years. Amber beads were even discovered in Britain, and are suggested to be at least ten thousand years old; dating all the way back to the end of the last ice age! The fact that these carefully designed beads travelled all the way to Great Britain shows just how valuable they were to the people of that era.

In this first chapter, I'm so excited to share with you the history of healing crystals, along with all gemstones and minerals that have made a mark on the world. But first, let me tell you why I love crystals so much. I've always had somewhat of an affinity for crystals and gems, starting at an early age.

When I was thirteen, I was visiting Boston, Massachusetts, I walked into my first ever New Age and crystal shop. I was immediately drawn to the table of crystals in the center of the shop. I don't know if it was the smell of sage or the warm and welcoming owner who helped me pick my first crystal, but that one experience sparked my love for using crystals and exploring new age practices. By the way, the crystal I chose was a rose quartz and it is still my favorite type of crystal.

As I got older, I started researching different stones and their meanings. I read any book I could find about holistic and alternative medicine and was surprised just how deep the history of precious stones and minerals ran in cultures around the world.

Personally, I don't think it's a coincidence that regardless of the time or region, every ancient civilization used these stones and defined their meanings. Especially when goods and word of mouth could only travel so far during ancient times. Now, I don't want to make this book about my own personal stone and crystal preferences and experiences, so let's dive right into the thick of it!

Scientists say that physical matter cannot be destroyed; it always remains on this Earth in one form or another. Crystals have always had a presence, and made their way into every region around the world. Martin Luther King jr. once said that we are not makers of history, but that we are made of history; and I think he's right.

Every event that has happened leading up to this moment, this time, has had an impact. We're not just a product of our own childhood and circumstance, but the result of millions of years of evolution, change, people, and decisions. It's amazing that something as old and meaningful as crystal healing, which was regularly practiced on a daily basis in so many cultures, has been shunned to the wayside because of modern beliefs and medicine.

Now, don't get me wrong. I truly believe in modern medicine, and that if someone is sick, then they should seek help from a medical professional. However, many conditions that are treated today with pills and medication were once healed with crystals, such as anxiety, skin disorders, lack of focus and depression.

While thousands of lives have been saved through new medical practices, I think there is a place in the world for both modern and traditional healing methods. Because of the fact of the matter is that the history of gemstones and crystals is woven deeply into our own. As we travel back thousands of years to explore the beginnings of crystal healing, consider just how influential these stones were to our development.

## Crystals and Stones Around the Globe

### Egypt

The very first historical references to the application if crystals come from the ancient Sumerians who actually used crystals to create magic formulas, specifically amber, which they thought was sunshine made solid. Colorful crystals were admired by Egyptians of all classes, but especially by those of royalty.

Egyptian kings, queens, and pharaohs are often depicted in grandeur and riches, with brilliant and colorful garments and accessories illustrating their status and wealth. Think of the way Cleopatra and Julius Caesar dressed. Regardless of the period or nation, jewels and vibrant garments were the epitome of wealth.

Ancient people wore jewelry that was typically made with lapis lazuli, carnelian, clear quartz, turquoise, and emerald. We all know that Egyptians were relatively curious in nature; I mean, have you ever researched the mummification process?

They soon began using these colorful stones and crystals for other things, one of them being makeup. For instance, galena and malachite were ground into a powder and then used as eyeshadow. I know that pharaohs and queens liked to dress up, but who knew that cosmetics dated all the way back to ancient Egypt?

A significant link to crystal use in Egyptian culture comes in the form of religion. No matter what religion you do or don't believe in, there's no denying the incredible and deep impact it played in shaping Egypt as a nation. The use of healing crystals is rooted in several legends, including extraterrestrial interference, a god/ gods, and even the migration of Atlantis priests from the lost city to Egypt. Egyptians carved grave amulets from precious and semi-precious stones.

They believed that the stones would help protect them from danger and improve their health. This is a common belief that you'll see across other cultures and the meaning they identify with certain crystals. Egyptians specifically used chrysolite, which was later translated to mean both topaz and peridot, to ward off night terrors and eradicate evil spirits, not surprising given their religious background. Egyptians took spirituality very seriously and would even make lapis into a poultice to be rubbed into the top of a person's head to remove spiritual impurities.

## Greece

The Ancient Greeks associated a number of properties to crystals, and many of the names that are used today for crystals and gems are actually of Greek origin. Even the word "crystal" derives from the Greek word for "ice." This is because the Greeks believed that clear quartz was actually water from the heavens that had become so frozen that it would stay in its solid state.

Amethyst translates to "not drunken" because it was used to prevent and treat drunkenness and hangovers. It really makes you wonder how intense parties must have been back then, and how innovative Greeks were in finding a hangover cure. On the other hand, according to Greek mythology, the drunken god of wine and rituals, Dionysus, had become infuriated with a young virgin named Amethyst.

Amethyst asked the goddess Diana for help and was turned into a dazzling white stone as protection. Upon realizing the damage of his actions, a remorseful Dionysus cried, and his tears fell into a cup of wine. When the cup accidentally spilled over, it covered the white stone, discoloring it into the crystal we know today as amethyst.

Amethyst isn't the only crystal with an origin in Greek mythology. The word "hematite" derives from the word for blood because the crystal turns a deep blood red when during oxidation. In Greek mythology, hematite is associated with Aries, the god of war. Similar to the Egyptian's thinking, Greek soldiers would rub hematite on their bodies before going into battle.

The significance of geology in Greece dates all the way back to the Classical Era, when silver, iron, gold, and other ore mines played a huge role in the structure of society. As a matter of fact, many of the famous monuments in Athens, such as the Parthenon, were built with the revenue generated from the mines. The Laviro silver mine in particular was a great source of wealth and influence in ancient Athens, and is considered analogous with the rise and fall of the Athenian Empire; dating from 5th to 4th B.C.

## China

Jade has always been a highly valued mineral in China, but the beginning of its influence in Chinese culture dates all the way back to ancient China. During that time, it was believed that the concentrated essence of love was in jade. It was also seen as a kidney- healing stone in China and South America.

Jade was used to make musical instruments, pendants symbolic of ancestor spirits, and burial armors for late emperors. Unlike other cultures, the Chinese language was influenced by stones (in this case, jade). Some of the Chinese characters were written to represent jade beads. Chinese culture was also influenced by other stones such as quartz, which was symbolic of the heart or essence of dragons and believed to have great power.

## India

India is the origin of many new age, holistic, and religious practices and traditions. Today, the country is one of the most reliable and richest sources for knowledge and instruction for crystals and their healing qualities. One of the oldest traditions in crystal healing comes from India; where placing crystals on chakras was an ancient practice. India also offers written documentation from 400 B. C. that contains information about some crystals and their ability to counteract negative influence from the planets and their positions.

It's incredibly interesting that ancient Indians used astrology as a significant explanation and map of how we live life on Earth; when culture in South American also prominently believed the same. In India, crystals were believed to possess emotional and spiritual powers. For example, moonstone was considered to be able to spark love, and onyx was thought to help relinquish ties of love. Above all, rubies were treasured the most and were considered to be the "king of precious stones."

## South America

I think we tend to forget the role that South America has played in humanity's systems of religion, spirituality, and medicine. The Western World is hailed as the king of modernism and advancement, while Eastern practices are respected for traditionalism and ties to the ways of the past. However, South America as a whole, although made up of many different countries with their own impact on the world, used crystals and precious stones too. Originally, crystals were used for ceremonial, healing, religious, and practical purposes throughout the continent.

Mayans would use the blackened volcanic glass, obsidian, to make ceremonial knives because they believed it would sharpen their vision in both the spiritual and physical realms. The Mayans would also use quartz, this time for medical purposes. They believed that crystals played a part in the consciousness of the earth, and would use quartz to diagnose and cure ailments with the planet's power.

Moving north to Mexico, the land was inhabited by Indian tribes. Ancient Mexicans would use the shiny gold mineral pyrite to make mirrors. From a religious standpoint, they believed that the souls of their ancestors who had led a good life would live inside the crystals.

## Scandanavia

Usually when you think of Vikings, you picture huge lumberjack-esque men with large beards wearing helmets with giant horns on either side. But these adventurous sailors and pillagers were also expert navigators; thanks to their handy dandy crystals.

From the 8th to the 11th centuries, Vikings fearlessly sailed the icy and uncharted seas, completely at the mercy of Mother Nature. They didn't have magnetic compasses and couldn't always navigate using the sun as a guide. Until recently, how the trailblazers traveled the open ocean at the time has been a complete mystery.

Archaeologists have evidence that proves Vikings transversed using portable wooden sundials. However, this tool could only have been used on clear sunny days. Sometimes while traveling along the Vikings' usual sailing routes, the sun would disappear for days at a time.

As unbelievable as it sounds, new research has suggested that the Vikings may have used crystals to find their way home. Norse sagas, compilations of writings from medieval Iceland, refer to a solarstein or "sunstone," which would exhibit unique properties when held up to the sky.

In 1967, archaeologist Thorkild Ramskou hypothesized that the crystals used by Vikings would show specific light patterns in the sky. These designs were caused by polarization, which would still be present even on overcast days and at night when the sun wasn't in the sky. The most prominent appearance of the sunstone, or "solarsteinn," can be found in a Viking saga about the legendary cultural hero Sigurd.

In one specific tale, King Olaf requests that Sigurd locates the sun through an impervious fog. To substantiate Sigurd's answer, which was correct, the King used a sunstone and looked at the sky to find where the light came from, correctly identifying the position of the sun.

Ramskou believed that the sunstones used were actually crystals, what would function as polarizing filters. By facing the stone towards the sky and rotating it until the sunbeams shining through the stone would reach the brightest point, it would be possible for the Vikings to successfully navigate the seas  using the sun. Although Ramskou's theory was widely accepted, there were skeptics who doubted the crystal's ability in overcast or foggy weather.

However, any lingering doubt was put to rest when a group of researchers from Hungary's Eotvos University published their research in an online journal. The team used a device that measures the degree of polarization of light, called a polarimeter, in adverse weather conditions to test Ramskou's theory. It turned out that the hypothesis was right on the money, with the patterns of the direction of polarization being undeniably clear.

What this research shows is that although there are so many people out there who doubt the use or benefits of crystals, we are still learning about our ancestors. And the truth of the matter is that crystals and stones were used all over the world for hundreds of years; and only now are we beginning to once again awaken and see just how important and helpful alternative medicine and tools are.

## Crystals in Religion

Okay friend, time to tackle the biggest misunderstanding and criticism of crystal healing: religion. I'm not going to lie; when I first started practicing crystal healing and really diving into the history or uses of crystals and stones, the harshest comments came from my friends and family who came from a more religious background. I'm also a religious person, don't get me wrong.

From my own personal research and investigation, I see the benefit of having both religion and alternative medicinal practices or traditions, because they both offer positive solutions. How my religious friends felt about crystal healing really came from a lack of understanding. Instead of viewing crystal use as an act of the devil or evil, they now see that crystals and gemstones have played a part in basically every religion.

Crystals and gemstones are mentioned throughout the Bible, Koran, and other religious documents and texts. For instance, the origin of birthstones actually comes from the breastplate of Aaron, described in the book of Exodus. And in the Koran, it's stated that the fourth heaven is made of carbuncle, or garnet. Hinduism also acknowledges the use of crystals through the Kalpa Tree.

The Kalpa Tree represents an offering to the Hindu gods, and is believed to be completely made of precious stone. Also, in a Buddhist document from the seventh century, it describes a beautiful grand throne made of diamond sitting underneath the Tree of Knowledge. It was on this throne that Buddhists believe a thousand Kalpa Buddhas lied down to rest and meditate.

Negative criticism for crystals and amulets were banned by the Christian church in 335 A. D., however gemstones still played vital roles within the religion. For example, saffire was the prefered gem for ecclesiastical rings in the twelfth century. In the eleventh century, Marbodus the Bishop of Rennes alleged that wearing agate would make the wearer more attractive, persuasive, and in God's favor.

There are many more symbolic references mentioned in the Bible and other religious texts, but I think you get the general idea. Although most people who practice religion don't believe in using crystals or other alternative methods, there is still just as much history of crystal use in religion as there is in cultures all over the world.

## The History of Crystal Healing

We've travelled around the world to learn about crystals in other cultures. Now it's time to dig a little deeper in the past. How did crystal use gain popularity? How did stones that were used on a regular basis become marked as tools of witchcraft and thrown to the wayside?

In similar fashion to how I went through the countries that have used crystals and gemstones in the past, I'm going to give you a brief overview of general stone and crystal use. Because I really want to show you the benefits of crystal healing, as well as how to use crystals and gemstones, and the many ways that you can use alternative practices to your advantage on a daily basis.

Let's start by travelling back to the Renaissance. The Renaissance is widely known as a turning point for humanity, with art, philosophy, science, and critical thinking coming to the forefront of culture. From the eleventh century and through the Renaissance, Europe produced several medical dissertations praising the moral excellence of precious and semi-precious stones in the treatment of specific ailments. During this time, stones were equally used with herbal remedies.

Writers such as Arnoldus Saxo and Hildegard von Binghen described stones with certain qualities of strength and even protection. It was these beliefs that in 1232 led Hubert de Burgh, the chief justicular of King Henry III, to steal a gem from the treasury and give it to the king of Wales, Henry III's enemy, to make him invincible in the fight for power. It's amazing how much scandal and conspiracy these little stones caused.

But if you think de Burgh's actions were dramatic, you'll see how seriously these stones and crystals were taken with this next historical fact. In Europe, it was believed that gemstones were actually corrupted by the original sins of Adam eating the forbidden fruit and lying to God. These sinful actions caused stones to become unclean, and possibly possessed by demons.

If compromised gems or crystals were handled by a sinner, that person's virtues would leave their body. It was this idea that created the act of cleansing or sanctifying crystals before wearing them - a tradition that is still practiced today in the crystal-using community!

It was German mathematician and scientist Johannes Kepler who started looking at crystals from a scientific point of view. His interest in crystals was sparked by a snowflake that landed on his coat, perfectly symmetrical and beautiful. In 1611, Kepler published a short essay called "Six-cornered Snowflake," which was the first mathematical characterization of crystals.

While this may seem like a far cry from the crystals that I'll be talking about in this book, just wait and see how influential this essay was. It was Kepler's writing that inspired Nicolaus Stensen, a Danish geologist, to write the cornerstone crystallographic Law of the Constancy of Interfacial Angles. Stensen observed that even though quartz and hematite come in various shapes and sizes, they each show the same interfacial angles regardless of their form.

This remark was confirmed even more than a hundred years later. What made Stenson's work even more remarkable even by modern standards, is that he showed the development of crystals through a fluid medium. Stenson's research on the growth of crystals greatly contributed to the advancement of crystallography.

Returning to a more fluid approach to crystal use (all puns intended), in 1609 during the same time that Kepler was studying crystals, Anselmus de Boot was making more spiritual claims of the properties of gemstones. He theorized that the properties or virtues of a gemstone were influenced by the presence of good or bad angels.

In this case, the good angles would provide a special grace to the user, while bad angels would tempt crystal users into believing that the stone itself possessed great powers on its own, rather than being bestowed with gifts by God. Within that same century, Thomas Nicols suggested that gems could not possess the remarkable effects claimed in the past, because stones and crystals are inanimate objects. This expression and the Age of Enlightenment began the slow downfall of gemstone and crystal use in Europe.

## Crystal Healing Today

Crystal healing has only recently come to practice again, in the 1980's with the beginning of New Age culture. Suddenly, using crystals and gemstones as healing methods was no longer a tradition of the past, but a curious practice that sparked new experimentation.

Books by Katrina Rafaell and Melody and Michael Gienger lead the way in popularizing crystals. Today, there are potentially thousands of books, articles, and magazines on the subject. Crystal healing made its way from alternative culture to widely acceptable as complementary therapy.

Crystal healing and other forms of alternative medicine have grounded roots primarily in larger cities. I'm not sure if it is the larger population or the bonding of many cultures in one space, but you can find crystal healing, chakra balancing, reiki, and other holistic treatment operations in almost every major city in the world. This leads me to my next major point in the final pages of this chapter.

Crystal healing is just one of many alternative holistic medical practices that can be found around the world. I feel that I wouldn't be doing this book topic justice if I didn't explain other practices that can positively change your life.

I know that there is noticeable stigma surrounding new-age medicine, and the only way to combat the misunderstandings and wrong information out there is to help educate those who are less familiar with these practices. So, before we continue forward on our crystal healing journey, take a look at some of the other healing methods that can positively impact your life.

## Alternative Holistic Medical Practices

Holistic medicine is a method of healing that doesn't just focus on the patient's physical state, but also their mind, spirit, and emotional wellbeing. Holistic medicine philosophy states that a person can achieve optimal health by maintaining proper balance in all areas. Holistic medicine professionals theorize that the entirety of a person is composed of interdependent parts; therefore, if one part is not functioning correctly, all the other areas will be affected as well.

To break it down on a more practical scale, think about how stress affects your overall state of being. Stress is an emotion that we feel, but it also affects our mental state with the inability to focus and overstimulation, as well as inhibiting our physical health. The physical effects of stress can range from extreme weight loss to weight gain, hair loss, and acne breakouts, just to name a few symptoms.

A holistic practitioner can use all forms of medicine to treat a patient, from conventional health care to alternative substitutes. One of the most common examples comes in the form of migraine headaches: a serious neurological condition that is accompanied by physical and neurological symptoms.

Rather than relying solely on heavy prescriptions, patients will seek help from holistic doctors who will investigate environmental triggers, diet and sleep habits, spiritual practices, and other potential health factors. Holistic doctors will evaluate your overall lifestyle in order to diagnose illnesses and treat them effectively. The belief that is the foundation of alternative medicine is that unconditional love and support are the most powerful treatments and that each person is solely responsible for their own health and being.

Holistic treatments begin with patient education on lifestyle and self- care modifications such as: diet, exercise, psychotherapy, spiritual counseling, acupuncture, chiropractor appointments, massage therapy, and homeopathy.

One area of holistic medicine that have slowly made its way to the forefront of new-age practices and common treatments is traditional alternative medicine. This area features forms of therapy that are more mainstream and widely accepted. Traditional alternative practices may include: homeopathy, acupuncture, naturopathy, Ayurveda, and Chinese/ oriental medicine.

There is also the belief of healing by touch, based off the belief that illness or painful injuries in one part of the body can affect all other areas. Therefore, touch is used as a form of therapy in hopes that with manual manipulation, all other parts of your body will be restored to full health so that your body can naturally dedicate more energy and effort into healing the one body part that hurts the most. Body-focused therapies include: chiropractic and osteopathic treatment, massages, tai chi, physical therapy, and yoga.

Diet and herbs have also played a significant role in both traditional and modern medical practices. Over the last few hundred years, the human diet has changed from a simple meat, fruit, vegetable, and grain diet to foods saturated in fats, carbohydrates, and added chemicals and unnecessary ingredients. Today's diet features both extreme excess and deficiency when it comes to nutritional value. Herbal and diet- based approaches work to balance the patient's nutritional well- being with: dietary supplements, herbal medicine, and overall diet manipulation.

The next type of holistic alternative medicine is founded on the belief of external energy; a belief that is similar to those who work with crystals. Practitioners of this type of treatment believe that outside energy from objects or other people directly influence a person's state of health. Forms of external energy therapy include: reiki, electromagnetic therapy, and qigong.

If you are looking for an alternative practice that also have scientific evidence to back it up, then look no further than your own mind. Both traditional and conventional medical professionals recognize the powerful connection between the body and the brain. There have been several studies that have shown that patients heal quicker and better if they are in good emotional and mental standing. Therapeutic treatments of the mind include: hypnosis, meditation, and biofeedback.

I hope that this short summary peaks your interest in exploring other types of healing practices. I won't get into the specifics, but I know that from personal experience certain therapies I mentioned have drastically changed my life and helped me make greater steps towards emotional, spiritual, and physical wellness. But enough about me, let's keep moving forward on learning more about crystal healing! This next chapter has a lot more in store!

# Chapter 2: Exploring Chakras and Charts

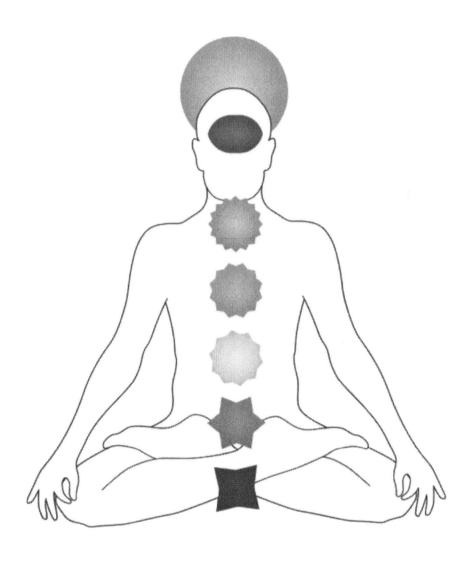

N ew Age medicine has slowly made its way back into popular culture. You may already be familiar with some of the terminology and even the functions of some practices. In this case, we are going to dive deep into the world of chakras. You may have heard about chakras if you've ever attended a yoga class or researched meditation.

In this chapter, I'm going to explain what exactly the chakras are, why they are important for your overall health and state of being, and how crystal healing is going to open and repair your chakras so that your positive energy can flow freely.

The word "chakra" comes from Sanskrit, and roughly translates to "wheel" or "disk." There are seven chakras within your body, each of them a spiritual centers that run from your feet all the way up to the top of your head. If you're already feeling skeptical about spiritual energy wells thriving inside your body, then take a look back through history. The chakra systems and charts originated in India sometime between 1500 and 500 B. C. in the oldest written text called "the Vedas."

The Vedas are the earliest Sanskrit records that hold most of the ancient scriptures and practices of Hinduism. The chakras correspond with your physical, mental, emotional, and spiritual states, which influence every part of your life.

Chakras contain "prana," which is pure healing energy that keeps us positive, healthy, and flourishing. Each of the seven chakras correlates with a specific region of the body, as well as spiritual elements that relate with the chakra.

## The Root Chakra

Your root chakra, also known as the first chakra, is the foundation of your body. When stimulated and balanced, the root chakra is supportive, grounded, and stabilizing. It keeps every other part of your spiritual and physical being connected and safe, so long as it is functioning efficiently. On a body chart, the root chakra is linked to the pelvic floor, base of the spine, and first three vertebrae.

It is also bonded to a person's sense of security and survival instincts. Due to the first chakra's spiritual and emotional connection in feelings of security and survival, it is also affiliated with whatever you use to ground yourself; including food, shelter, safety mechanisms, and fears of letting go and finding safety. When the root chakra is blocked, it can result in a variety of ailments such as anxiety disorders, nightmares, and increased feelings of fear. On a physical level, the root chakra is directly connected to issues with the colon, lower back, feet, bladder, and legs.

# The Sacral Chakra

The second chakra is located right above the pelvic bone, underneath your belly button. Considering the placement of this second chakra, you may have already guessed what it is responsible for. That's right, the sacral chakra is connected to your sexual and creative energies. This chakra is identified with the color orange and the element of water. When your sacral chakra is balanced, you will feel friendlier, happier, more passionate, more fulfilled and successful, and overly abundant.

Sounds like all of your problems and insecurities will go away, right? You can align the sacral chakra by honoring your body, creatively expressing yourself, and staying fluid and positive in your energy. When your second chakra is blocked, you will feel uninspired, emotionally unstable, and depressed. On a physical level, you may experience sexual dysfunction, afraid of change, and exhibit addictive behaviors.

# The Solar Plexus Chakra

Solar plexus translates to "lustrous gem: in Sanskrit. This third chakra is a flowing spring of empowerment and self-esteem. The solar plexus chakra dictates your action and balance, with willpower, individual power, and commitment strengthening as energy flows through it. The third chakra is located between the navel and rib cage.

On a physical level, it regulates your metabolism, digestive tract, and stomach. When your third chakra is blocked or not functioning as well as it should, you will suffer from indecisiveness, low self- esteem, procrastination, and feelings of anger and the need to control everything around you. The solar plexus chakra isn't just regulatory of your self-esteem, but also how you act on the outside; expressing apathy and being taken advantage of more easily.

## The Heart Chakra

If you're dealing with negativity towards others and having a difficult time with personal romantic relationships, then it's time to look inward towards your heart chakra. The fourth chakra is also known as the central chakra. It lies within the center of your chest, where the spiritual and physical realms meet.

On a physical level, it is believed that the central chakra epitomizes the heart, lungs, breasts, and thymus gland. Spiritually and emotionally, the heart chakra has all about love, spiritual awareness, service to others, and forgiveness.

This chakra is identified with the colors green and pink. When open and balanced, the central chakra allows love and compassion to flow freely with positive energy. However, when it is blocked, the heart chakra will submit to feelings of betrayal, anger, grief, hatred, and jealousy.

## The Throat Chakra

Your fifth chakra is all about speaking your truth properly and proudly. Chances are, this chakra is well- balanced compared to your other chakras. It rules over all communication and is the first of the three spiritual chakras. The spiritual chakras are solely spiritual, while the other four lower chakras tend to manifest themselves physically. Your throat chakra affects your parathyroid, neck, thyroid, mouth, larynx, and tongue.

When the fifth chakra is balanced and open, you will find that you can listen to others with more openness and consideration, as well as talk and clearly express yourself openly. When this chakra is closed off, you will find it difficult to pay attention, stay focused, speak in congruence with your true self, and be hindered by a fear of judgment from the people around you. If your fifth chakra is not working efficiently, it will reveal itself in the form of a sore throat, neck and shoulder pain, thyroid problems, and headaches.

The third- eye chakra is not to be confused with the third chakra. The third-eye chakra is the sixth chakra and lies between your eyebrows. The third eye rules over the pituitary gland, head, eyes, and lower half of the brain. Your third eye guides your intuition; the more you tap into it, the easier it will be to recognize what your true self is trying to communicate. The third-eye chakra is a powerful bridge between your authentic self and the physical world.

It allows you to see through the drama and walls that are in the physical world to clearly see the intentions of others around you. When your sixth chakra is blocked, you will find it difficult to connect with your own intuition, trust your truth, remember important facts, and have trouble learning new things. Your third-eye chakra is inherently connected with all of your lower chakras.

So, if your third-eye is unbalanced, the rest of your chakras will be as well. Emotional and physical issues correlated with your sixth chakra include: anxiety, depression, dismissiveness, introverted behavior, judgmental thoughts, headaches, dizziness, and neurological disorders.

# The Crown Chakra

In Sanskrit, the crown seventh chakra is known as the Sahasrara chakra; which translates to the "thousand petal lotus." Your crown chakra is the center of spiritual enlightenment and is the ultimate spiritual connection to your highest self and the divine.

The crown chakra is located at the top of your head. When it is balanced, you will experience full spiritual awareness, higher consciousness, undivided focus and attention, and the ability to expand your mind further than thought possible. When the seventh chakra is blocked, you may experience feelings of distress, loneliness, and disconnected from the people and things around you.

On the other hand, when your crown chakra is off-balance, you may just feel like your normal self; this isn't necessarily a bad thing, but you won't feel like you're in an elevated state of spiritual enlightenment. You can open your crown chakra by practicing yoga or other meditative exercises. It is difficult to achieve a state of complete self-awareness through an open crown chakra, but you can get a taste of it by practicing moments of prayer or gratitude every day to enjoy moments of spiritual connection.

# Balancing Your Chakras with Healing Crystals

Every one of your seven chakras are strongly connected to certain colors, foods, and as you may have already guessed, crystals and gemstones. In a modern world that thrives off of constant intense energy, stimulation, and busy schedules, it is incredibly easy for your energy field to become unbalanced.

However, you can realign your chakras with healing crystals. Colorful healing crystals create certain vibrations that will balance and cleanse your chakras so your energy can vibrate at a higher frequency and live in congruence with your highest self.

The first and easiest way to balance your chakras, or at the very least start opening them, is to pay attention to how you react to stressful situations. Look at your life closely; if you are experiencing recurring issues or illnesses, it could be because one of your chakras is out of alignment.

For example, I had a friend who was overwhelmed and stressed out at work because her boss was taking advantage of her work ethic. She didn't want to cause trouble and create more distress at work, so she kept her feelings to herself like so many of us do.

Soon, she found that everytime she would be near her boss, her throat would get painfully sore and close up so that she couldn't speak. She realized that she wasn't speaking her truth, and when she finally found the courage to act in congruence with her highest self, she talked to her boss and had instant relief.

That is how powerful our chakras are and how important it is to keep them balanced and freely flowing with energy. You already know the chakras and what they do. The next step is learning which crystals will help each of your chakras.

## The Root Chakra

The first chakra located at the base of your spine is associated with the color red. The root chakra enhances your sense of security, feeling grounded, and a confidence in your identity; and all of these feelings are elevated by root chakra crystals. You can use red garnet, red jasper, smoky quartz, hematite, and black onyx.

## The Sacral Chakra

Your second chakra lies in your lower abdomen and is correlated with the color orange. The sacral chakra is connected to feelings of sexuality, personal empowerment, creativity, and passion. These attributes are elevated with goldstone, tiger's eye, amber, orange calcite, and carnelian.

## The Solar Plexus Chakra

Your third chakra is based behind your navel, deep within your diaphragm, and it is connected to hues of yellow. The solar plexus chakra is in control of your honor, courage, and compassion towards others. The healing crystals associated with the solar plexus chakra are yellow jade, pyrite, citrine, and rutilated quartz.

## The Heart Chakra

Your fourth chakra is positioned in the center of your chest and is related to the colors green and pink. Your heart chakra inspires you to live from the heart and connect with yourself and others in ways that your lower chakras just can't do. You can open up your heart chakra by using emerald, green calcite, amazonite, rose quartz, aventurine, and chrysoprase.

## The Throat Chakra

Your fifth chakra is centered just above the collar bone and throat area, and is influenced by the color blue. The throat chakra encourages truth, honest living, communication, and self - expression. All of these can be enhanced with sodalite, aquamarine, angelite, kyanite, and apatite.

## The Third- Eye Chakra

Your third- eye chakra rests just above the eyebrows and is strengthened by the color purple. The sixth chakra is responsible for your intuition, self-actualization, guidance, and self- discipline. You can use amethyst, iolite, angelite, fluorite, and charoite to balance your third- eye chakra.

## The Crown Chakra

Your crown chakra, as you may have guessed, is located right at the top of your head and has a strong connection to the colors white and purple. The seventh chakra is arguably the most important, as it promotes the balance and energy flowing from the other chakras. The crown chakra influences spirituality, profound thinking, and meditation. To heal your crown chakra, use amethyst, blue lace agate, clear quartz, ametrine, and lepidolite.

# How to Balance Your Chakras

The easiest way to activate and heal your chakras is using crystal jewelry. Now that you know all about the chakras and the crystals that are associated with each one, you can incorporate a combination of stones to promote healing and transformation.

The moment these stones come into contact with your body, they imbue your mind, body, and spirit with their cleansing and curative abilities. Healing your chakras with crystals is all about taking action to ensure that your energy is secure and anchored while giving you the inspiration you need to take massive leaps forward in your life.

Another simple method for rebalancing the chakras is with a full body chakra cleanse. You can start by using a chakra chart as a guiding reference. Start by placing a gemstone on each of your seven chakras, starting at the crown chakra and placing a crystal on the root chakra last.

Although I listed several different stones to use for your first chakra, I personally recommend using smoke quartz at the bottom of your feet and around your sides and head. Doing this creates a protective perimeter around your energy, which will block out any negative energy. The powerful cleansing energy will also increase the strength of the other stones.

As the crystals cleanse your chakras, focus on gently breathing in a steady rhythm. Then with your eyes closed, visualize a white light illuminating the stones and radiating out, flowing into your chakras. Stay in this position physically and mentally for fifteen to twenty minutes. You can also use sound frequencies to help deepen your mental state and intensify your focus. There are also YouTube videos you can look up that will guide you through the meditation process.

Although you may not be able to physically see your chakras, you can feel them with your intuition. After all, who knows your body better than you? As you meditate while using the crystals, practice mindfulness in turning your energy inward and using your inner sight.

A balanced and healthy chakra will spin rapidly and smoothly. The colors will appear clear and bright. If one of your chakras is off-balance, it will spin too fast or too slow and the colors can appear to be faded and fragmented. Starting with the first chakra and working your way up to the crown chakra, focus on your chakra's color, size, and speed as it transforms and heals.

## Using Crystal Grids

Crystal grids are one of the most powerful ways of clarifying and manifesting your goals, dreams, and intentions. A crystal grid derives its power from the combined energies of the crystals you put on it. A crystal grid is a specific arrangement of gems and crystals that, when coupled with intentions, will make your goals or desires manifest into becoming reality.

I'm going to show you how to lay your crystals out on a grid so that you can start using your crystals and stones to generate the energy that can bring healing and prosperity to your life. Just don't forget that the universe doesn't just give you want you want, it gives you what you need.

Now, you might be wondering what the difference is between using individual crystals and using a crystal grid. The power that comes from using a crystal grid is created by uniting the energies between healing stones, sacred geometry, and your focused intentions. The consolidation of the energy from the crystals and the geometric patterns contributes an added strength to manifest your intentions faster than with an individual stone.

Think of using crystal grids like you would create a vision board. You can have multiple grids at home, each designed to manifest specific goals or desires. There aren't rules set in stone for using crystal grids. With crystal healing in general, it's usually always best to use your own instincts to guide you.

Some people like to use a cloth or piece of paper with sacred symbols on them, as this can increase the power of the crystals. You can also use things found in nature, like leaves or flowers. The stones you use can be chosen based on the properties they individually offer in order to get the most out of your grid. The possibilities are truly endless when it comes to creating a crystal grid.

## Making a Crystal Grid

**Step 1:** The first step in making a crystal grid is deciding what your intentions are for it. You can write down your intention or goal on a piece of paper and put it under the central stone in the grid. You want to be as specific as possible with your goals, and think about what you need, not just what you want.

**Step 2:** Pick your crystals. You already know what crystals effect which chakras. Keeping your intentions in mind, use your instincts and knowledge to choose the crystals that will help manifest your intentions. Or you can also just use whatever crystals you have on hand.

**Step 3:** Cleanse your crystals and the space you are doing your crystal grid in before creating the grid. Later on in the next chapter, I'll go more in-depth on how to clean and care for your crystals. However, a stick of sage, moonlight, or sound are just a few methods for cleansing your crystals.

**Step 4:** Put the piece of paper you wrote your intentions on in the center of your space. As you do this, either out loud or just in your mind, declare what your intentions are. Take a minute to slow down your breathing, and focus on connecting with your true self and the energy radiating from the universe. I find that lighting a candle and playing music softly in the background helps keep me centered while I create my crystal grids.

**Step 5:** When forming the rest of the grid, the processes will depend on your own personal preference. Some people believe that starting from the outside and working your way in is better, while others start from the center and work their way towards the outside. You can use your intentions when placing your crystals or refer to sacred geometry to create your grid. Using a guide is also an easy way to get started with using crystal grids if you're new to the practice.

**Step 6:** Now, it's finally time to activate your grid! I prefer to use some type of quartz tower or wand to draw an invisible "connect the dots" between the crystals. As you touch each crystal with the point your activating crystal, you are creating an invisible connection from one crystal to another. In my experience, it's best to leave the grid in place for a couple of days instead of putting it away as soon as you're done. I like to leave my crystal grids up for about three days, but it all comes down to what your intuition tells you. Regardless, they make a beautiful addition to any room.

## Crystal Shapes and Structures

Crystals have a unique effect on us - even though each person individually finds themselves drawn to specific colored stones. We share an inherent desire to collect and carry these beautiful gems, because their energy influences ours and somehow makes a difference in our lives and the way we feel. But the color of a crystal is not the only characteristic that matters.

There are special meanings, properties, and uses of crystal shapes: such as pyramids, hearts, skulls, spheres, and angels. In this next section, I'm going to break down the meaning behind the most common crystal shapes that you will find a crystal or new age shop. However, keep in mind that these are cut and polished crystals, not their natural form.

Carving and shaping crystals into symbols or shapes is an ancient practice. Tracing the history and origins of crystal healing back to ancient civilizations like the Romans, Egyptians, and Chinese, you can find that they all used natural crystals as well as carved crystals and gemstones.

While it is clear that crystals were considered effective and sacred objects, why carve them at all? When a crystal is carved into a specific shape, it enhances some properties or even adds new ones to the gem. Crystals that are cut add an aesthetic appeal to the stone, but it also enables the user to work with the crystal in other ways. Carving a shape directs the crystal's energy in a different way.

When choosing a crystal shape, you need to decide what exactly it will be used for. Keep in mind that all crystals have natural powers that will always maintain their properties regardless of what shape they come in. It's always a good idea to stick with your intuition, but you should still research the properties of both the crystal and its shape even if you are drawn to a specific shape.

# A Tumble Stone

A tumbled stone crystal is the most common cut and polished form that you can find. Tumbled stones are small, round, polished crystals. They are made using a machine called a rock tumbler, which will tumble the tiny stones until their edges are smooth. Their shapes and sizes will vary, but the form itself is a "one size fits all" use.

The crystal's energy will radiate in multiple directions. What makes tumble stones so great, especially for someone who is newer to crystal healing, is that you can carry them in a pocket or purse, keep them at home or the office, and place them directly on your body, chakra, or crystal grid. As a bonus, they are also more affordable than other cuts.

# A Pyramid Crystal

Pyramid crystals have four triangular sides and a square bottom. What makes a pyramid shape ideal is that it anchors and directs energies. It stabilizes the energies from the earth while also enhancing and projecting them out of the pinnacle.

You can use small crystal pyramids on chakras to rebalance them, or place them around your home to create a centered and balanced environment. Pyramids are powerful central stones in crystal grids, capable of raising vibrations and heightening your intentions.

A crystal sphere is exactly what fortune tellers and gypsies in movies and books are referring to when they use a "crystal ball." Crystal spheres are cut, shaped, and polished into a perfectly round ball. They emanate energy smoothly and evenly in every direction. They also have the special property of neutralizing negative or unbalanced energizes. A unique property of crystal spheres is that they are not only connected to the earth, but also other planets and the moon.

They also specifically help in opening the third-eye chakra. Sphere-shaped crystals were traditionally used for fortune telling, also known as scrying. They can be held over chakras and auras for energy healing. Although spheres will need a stand to be displayed in your home, but they instill a sense of peace and grounded energy. You can place them in the center of a crystal grid to promote healing, protection, and psychic growth.

## A Heart Crystal

As you may have already guessed, heart-shaped crystals symbolize love, your heart, and the connection with the heart chakra. Crystals that are cut and shaped into hearts can be placed directly over your heart chakra to heal it.

Small hearts are ideal for carrying with you to keep you centered wherever you go. Larger heart-shaped crystals can be placed around your home or work, and used with crystal grids. It is believed that crystal hearts attract love and new relationships. They also heal broken hearts and emotional wounds.

## A Standing Point

Different from a pyramid, a standing crystal point is also known as a crystal tower. A crystal tower is cut into a point with a machine, or can be made with natural formation by simply cutting the crystal at the base to let it stand on its own.

Similar to other pointed crystals, a tower will direct and focus energy out of the peak of the stone. Towers are typically cut into generator points so that your energy and intentions are magnified. A crystal tower is recommended for gridding the corners of a room, and are often used as the central stone in a crystal grid.

## A Crystal Angel

Crystal angels can be found in many sizes. They are not designed to be realistic statues and are usually on the smaller side of shaped crystals. Crystals that are shaped into angels anchor angelic positive energies, which will help connect you with your guardian angels. Placing angels around your home or in your car will provide a higher vibration, protection, and healing. They can also be used as the center crystal in a grid.

## A Crystal Wand

Although less common than other formations, a crystal wand can be found in many shapes and sizes. A wand is made out of a solid piece of crystal that is cut into a point. Crystal wands are also referred to as massage wands. They are typically used to direct the energy of the crystal into an aura or chakra. They are also popular tools for those who practice reiki and energy healing. As a small bonus to using crystal wands, the rounded end or fattest end of the wand can be used to ward off negative energy.

Even though I focused on repairing chakras and building crystal grids in this chapter, these are only two of the many ways to heal yourself and others by using crystals. However, a lot of the ailments and negative feelings that we experience are largely due to imbalanced chakras or not clearing our intentions and living congruently with our highest self.

In the following chapter, we're going to jump into the deep end of crystal healing. You already know how to use healing crystals like a pro, now it's time for the best part - choosing your crystals!

Much like other holistic and alternative medical practices, crystal healing is not just about physical well-being, but mental, emotional, and spiritual as well. It's one of the most efficient practices that you can adopt for overall health and prosperity; and I'm going to show you exactly how to achieve that.

# CHAPTER 3: CHOOSING YOUR CRYSTALS

There is no such thing as having too many crystals! They come in dozens of shapes, sizes, and colors; all of which greatly impact the power and effectiveness of the crystal. If you're new to crystal healing and new age practices, it can be overwhelming and confusing trying to find the crystals that are right for you and your needs. This is especially true now that the internet plays such a huge part in our lives.

While the web makes it easier for us to learn about subjects we care about and connect with people who have similar interests, it also leads to unverified sources and vendors who sell fake crystals to unsuspecting consumers. My goal in this chapter is to make the crystal choosing experience for you that much better. Because whether or not you have access to a new age store, or have to resort to internet vendors, you should have a clear idea of what type of crystal you want, what you're going to use it for, and how to care for it.

## Choosing a Crystal

Crystals are undoubtedly beautiful, but they are more than just for show. Every crystal and gemstone has special rare properties and vibrations that can be used to heal. In this section, I'm going to show you how to choose the right crystal for your desires and intentions.

### Call onto the crystal that is best for you.

The best way to get something you want is to just ask! Openly ask the universe to direct you towards the crystal that will work for your highest self and your greatest needs. Remember to keep an open mind and reserve any judgement towards any crystal that may cross your path.

You may have preconceived notions about the type of crystal you need to empower you, and end up with something completely different. Regardless, the best and easiest way to select a healing crystal is to choose an area of your life that you want to change or improve, and then use your instincts to select a crystal that resonates with those desires.

Keep in mind that every crystal has unique powers that can influence your energy field in many ways. There are crystals to match every intention; whether it's protection and confidence, self- development, health and positivity, the list goes on. Once you have defined your intention, you can move forward with selecting a crystal.

## *Wait to have a physical reaction to a crystal.*

Sometimes, we can't define our intentions or we don't even know what we want - and that's okay. Crystals and gemstones will still work even if we can't identify what we need to ask or search for. Working with crystals is a form of connecting directly with the universe.

They align us with the intentions of our true selves even if we are having trouble connecting to our higher consciousness. The physical world can cloud your judgement and influence your desires, so that you become disassociated with who you really are and what you really want.

If you aren't instinctively attracted to a crystal, try waiting for a physical reaction. You can do this by closing your eyes, taking your non- dominant hand and passing it over a selection of crystals. Wait to see if you feel a subtle tingling or tug from one of the stones. You may end up feeling drawn to more than one crystal; in which case, you would move onto the third method of choosing a crystal.

## Experiment with different stones.

Another way of choosing your crystal is to find one that directly correlates with what you want to heal. Later on in this chapter, there will be a detailed list of different crystals to choose from and their properties. You can also use the internet, a new age guidebook, or your chakra knowledge for guidance. If you are shopping for crystals at a new age store, you can ask to see stones that relate to a particular chakra or simply buy whichever stones you're drawn to and use them to see which one works best for you needs.

## Using your astrological sign as a guide.

Last, but definitely not least, you can use your astrological sign to guide you in choosing a crystal. There are twelve zodiac signs, one of which is associated to your date of birth. If you don't really have a clear purpose in using a crystal and simply want to experiment with them in general, referencing your astrological sign may be the perfect way to start.

**Aries (March 21st - April 19th) -** Aries are naturally ambitious and driven, they also make great leaders. Stones that resonate most with those born under Aries are citrine, carnelian, green jasper, and bloodstone.

**Taurus (April 20th - May 20th) -** If you're born under the Taurus sign, you're naturally loyal, predictable, and dependable. Taureans are well-grounded and devoted to their loved ones. The stones that align with Taureans are amber, jade, malachite, and dioptase.

**Gemini (May 21st - June 20th) -** Those born under the Gemini astrological sign can be quick-witted, great communicators, and quick to adapt to new situations. A few crystals that are associated with Gemini are watermelon tourmaline, labradorite, chrysoprase, and agate.

**Cancer (June 21st - July 22nd) -** Cancerians are compassionate, tenacious, emotional, and persuasive people. The stones that best align with their nature are red jasper, emerald, moonstone, and pearl.

**Leo (July 23rd - August 22nd) -** Leos are incredibly confident, vibrant, warm, and passionate. A Leo's energy is magnified by carnelian, golden topaz, onyx, and pyrite.

**Virgo (August 23rd - September 22nd) -** People born under the zodiac sign of Virgo are practical, kind, determined, and work hard to help the people they care about. Crystals that resonate the most with Virgos are green jade, blue tourmaline, moss agate, and peridot.

**Libra (September 23rd - October 22nd) -** Librans are cut from an artistic cloth. They are fun, smart, social, and diplomatic. Librans are typically drawn to peridot, opal, tourmaline, and sodalite.

**Scorpio (October 23rd - November 21st) -** If you fall under the star sign of Scorpio, then you are most likely a passionate, charismatic, independent, and resourceful person. A Scorpio's energy is best matched with aquamarine, malachite, rhodochrosite, smoky quartz, and topaz.

**Sagittarius (November 22nd - December 21st) -** Sagittarians are generous, sociable, idealistic, and have a great sense of humor. Crystals that align with the energy of a Sagittarius are tiger's eye, sodalite, topaz, and turquoise.

**Capricorn (December 22nd - January 19th) -** Capricorns are ambitious, disciplined, responsible, and strong-willed. Some stones that best resonate with Capricorns are fluorite, malachite, hematite, and tiger's eye.

**Aquarius (January 20th - February 18th) -** Those who fall within the Aquarius astrological sign are honest and independent. Crystals that are connected with Aquarians are amethyst, turquoise, garnet, and opal.

**Pisces (February 19th - March 20th) -** Pisces are known for being loyal, putting their friendships first, and dedicating their lives towards achieving goals and making their dreams come true. A few stones that resonate with a Pisces are amethyst, angelite, sapphire, and aquamarine.

## Choosing a Crystal with a Purpose

| Crystal | Purpose & Properties | Physical Effects | Aligning Chakra |
|---|---|---|---|
| Agate | Courage and Strength Agate brings physical and emotional strength. It helps in pursuing acceptance of oneself and | Healing emotional tension, alleviate digestive issues, and relieving skin disorders. | Third-Eye & Crown |

| | | | |
|---|---|---|---|
| | seeking your truth. Agate's healing qualities will soothe your mind, body, and spirit. | | |
| Amethyst | Peace and Spirituality Amethyst is the crystal of stability, inner peace, spirituality, and strength. For those who practice meditation, it is the perfect stone for heightening your intuition and psychic abilities. It brings clarity, understanding, and greater conscious perception. | Relieving insomnia, reducing stress, easing headaches, strengthening the immune system, reducing inflammation, and assisting the pituitary gland. | Third-Eye & Crown |

| | | | |
|---|---|---|---|
| Ametrine | Optimism Ametrine is the perfect and powerful combination of citrine and amethyst. It has high energy, which reduced stress, tension, and emotional blockages. It can be used to connect with your highest consciousness and brings protection and focus during astral travel. | Effective in treating long-standing ailments, relieving depression and fatigue, alleviating headaches and stress. | Solar Plexus, Third-Eye, & Crown |
| Amazonite | Intuition and Hope Amazonite is the stone of hope and intuition. It is best used to filter outside noise so that you can focus | Increasing brain power, memory, and focus, improving the nervous system. | Heart |

| | | | |
|---|---|---|---|
| | on what your true self is trying to tell you. This stone can also be used to strengthen faith, enhance masculinity, and increase physical strength. | | |
| Angelite | Awareness Angelite helps in providing clear and honest communication. It encourages speaking with compassion and expressing your truth. Angelite also promotes contact with the angelic realm while staying grounded with the reality of everyday life. | Supporting bone density, treating arthritis, and promoting the healing of fractured bones. | Throat |
| Apophyllite | Identifying Truth | Alleviating | Heart & |

| | | | |
|---|---|---|---|
| | The crystal apophyllite generates conscious access between the physical and spiritual realms; allowing you to connect to past life experiences. It helps you to identify and act in accordance with the truth, regardless of the situation. This crystal promotes spiritual and emotional calm, and be used to open your third-eye chakra to bring light and positive energy into your heart. | suppressed emotions, promoting deep relaxation, relieving anxiety, fear, and doubt, and aiding treatment for respiratory ailments. | Third-Eye |
| Aragonite Sputnik | Patience & Reliability Aragonite sputnik | Aids in treating nerve and muscle spasms, | Root |

| | | | |
|---|---|---|---|
| | increases your patience and acceptance to take on additional responsibility. As a grounding crystal, it clears stressful blockages and enhances reliability and resourcefulness. | restores damaged bones and discs. | |
| Aquamarine | Clarity & Purity This crystal has the power to purify your body, as well as promote clarity of mind and enhance compassionate and positive energy. It will help bring closure to unresolved issues, promote courage, and take away your fears | Calms the nerves, reduces bloating, eases sore throats, strengthens the liver, pituitary gland, thyroid gland, and kidneys. | Throat & Aligning all Chakras |

| | | | |
|---|---|---|---|
| | and self- doubt. It is the stone for meditation and physical, emotional, and mental balance. | | |
| Blue Lace Agate | Communication & Purity<br><br>Blue lace agate will help to open and expand your consciousness, stimulate intuition and spiritual acumen. It will encourage creativity, self-expression, and harmonious communication with others. It will also reduce stress and bring peace of mind. Blue lace agate is a nurturing stone that will give you patience, honesty, | Healing sore throats, reducing bloating, healing blockages in the nervous system, relieving neck and shoulder tension, treating fevers, and arthritis pain. | Heart & Throat |

| | | | |
|---|---|---|---|
| | wisdom, and positivity. | | |
| Blue Quartz | **Harmony & Calming** This crystal will purify you both physically and emotionally. It will bring peace of mind, encourage self-expression, and stimulate healthy relationships. It stimulates intuition, communication, and creativity. | Relieving stress and negativity, healing throat ailments, purifying the blood. | Throat & Third Eye |
| Calcite (Clear) | **Cleanses & Amplifies** Clear calcite is a powerful energy amplifier and cleanser, which will bring you joy, positivity, and a sense of grounding. It will | Strengthening teeth, bones, and joints, detoxing the organs, treating skin conditions, healing damaged tissue, strengthening the immune | All Chakras |

| | | | |
|---|---|---|---|
| | balance out unsteady emotions, relieve stress, and boost focus and memory. Clear calcite is used to bring confidence and trust in yourself. It will inhibit laziness and naturally stimulate your energy and drive to get things done. | system, and relieving stress. | |
| Calcite (Golden) | **Joy & Lightheartedness** Just like clear calcite, golden calcite will amplify and cleanse your positive energy. It increases trust in oneself, brings emotional balance, enhances | Aiding digestion and enhancing the metabolism, strengthening the teeth and bones, detoxing the organs, and healing damaged tissue and skin disorders. | Sacral, Solar Plexus, & Crown |

| | | | |
|---|---|---|---|
| | your memory, and alleviates stress. Golden calcite is the perfect stone to use for meditation, allowing your mind to reach higher planes and connect your emotions with intellect. | | |
| Carnelian | Joy & Warmth This crystal brings warmth and joy to overflow your highest self with radiating positivity. It is the stone to use for increasing your motivation, restoring vitality, and inspiring creativity. Carnelian will | Increasing circulation and blood flow, stimulating the metabolism, helping tissue regeneration, healing the lungs, kidneys, liver, and pancreas. This particular stone is also known to aid overcoming abuse. | Sacral, Solar Plexus, & Heart |

| | | | |
|---|---|---|---|
| | give you courage and insight to make the right decisions in life choices. It increases your willpower, focus, and trust in yourself. | | |
| Celestite | Positivity & Uplifting The crystal celestite will radiate calm, uplifting energy. It brings harmony to your life and will help to reveal the truth and resolve conflict in sticky situations. Celestite is one of the best crystals to place in your bedroom, as it will clear away negative energy and bring soft | Brining quick relief to pain, treating eye and ear disorders, detoxing the body, alleviating chronic tension, healing damaged bones, tissue, and organs. | Throat & Crown |

| | | | |
|---|---|---|---|
| | positive energy to your most sacred environment. Promoting purity of heart, it will help you access the angelic realm to lead you towards enlightenment. | | |
| Chevron Amethyst | Intuition & Spirituality Chevron amethyst has many of the properties that amethyst offers, such as inner peace, strength, enhancing intuition and psychic abilities. Amethyst will give you clarity and an enhanced understanding and conscious perception. Chevron amethyst | Stimulating the immune system, enhancing the connection and balance between the organs. | Third - Eye & Crown |

| | | | |
|---|---|---|---|
| | will provide the additional powers of purity, calmness, and positive problem solving in difficult situations. | | |
| Citrine | Cleansing & Revitalizing As the name suggests, citrine is an energizing crystal that promotes happiness, hope, and courage. Citrine is believed to hold the energy of the sun, and therefore increases your self-esteem and creativity. It is a revitalizing crystal used to awaken the body, mind, and spirit. It is frequently | Healing the digestive system and heart, relieving infection, aiding tissue regeneration, detoxing both the physical, emotional, and mental bodies. It is also the perfect stone to use for relieving menstrual pain and symptoms, as well as bringing balance to hormones. | Solar Plexus & Crown |

| | | | |
|---|---|---|---|
| | used to attract good fortune and prosperity into one's life. | | |
| Clear Quartz | Energizing Clear quartz will bring balance and energy to all areas of your life, as well as your mind and body. This particular crystal is used in meditation to direct energies with more intensity. It will strengthen the connection with your higher self to allow spiritual guidance as you move forward in your life. Clear quartz is used to improve memory and focus, as well as provide clarity. | Soothing and treating burns, stimulating the immune system, bringing balance to uneasy emotions, and stimulating the pineal and pituitary glands. | All Chakras |

| | | | |
|---|---|---|---|
| Desert Rose/ Selenite | Possibility & Opportunity It is believed that the desert rose stones are carved by the souls of the Native American Indians. Desert rose intensifies love and teamwork, and encourages you to go after your goals without fear or self- doubt. This crystal is used to reaffirm your purpose in life. | Aligning the spinal column, promoting flexibility, soothing the nerves, and aiding treatments for epilepsy. | Crown |
| Epidote | Regeneration Epidote is a unique crystal. It is known to affect people in different ways, depending on the energy the individual is | Encouraging recovery and regeneration after illness, resolving feelings of sadness, grief, and sorrow. | Heart |

| | | | |
|---|---|---|---|
| | transmitting. Basically, whatever energy you are putting out, epidote will increase it. Used with positivity and open-mindedness, it can bring enlightenment and a greater connection with your higher self. | | |
| Fire Agate | Protection & Courage Fire agate will bring you protection, strength, and courage. It has a connection to the earth, which translates to feelings of security and safety. Fire agate promotes | Overcoming addictions, relieving stomach and intestine issues, treating chronic inflammation, and aiding circulatory and nervous disorders. | Solar Plexus & Sacral |

| | | | |
|---|---|---|---|
| | motivation, commitment, and understanding. It will also relieve cravings and temptations. | | |
| Fluorite | Protection & Focus The crystal fluorite improves focus, understanding, and clear unbiased decision making. It is often used in meditation due to its ability to advance the mind and aid in interdimensional transmissions. It is a protective crystal that cleanses the mind and body, removes negative energy, and | Strengthening your teeth and bones helping treat spine and arthritic conditions, defending against common colds and the flu, treating infectious diseases, and aiding in resolving emotional trauma. | Third-Eye |

| | | | |
|---|---|---|---|
| | defends your spirit from outside influences. | | |
| Green Aventurine | Tranquility Green aventurine is used to encourage positivity, joy, emotional balance, and the balancing of both male and female energies. Aventurine has the power of promoting compassion and empathy, as well as stimulating independence and motivation. It also protects the user against electromagnetic energy and outside pollution. | Aiding in the healing of muscles and bones, soothing headaches and migraines, lowering blood pressure, relieving anxiety and stress, protecting against heart disease, and treating sleep disorders. | Heart |
| Green Jade | Emotional | Strengthening | Heart |

|  | Balance Green jade balances your emotions, and brings nurturing, peace, and purity into your life. It has the power to remove negative energy, while radiating love, serenity, wisdom, and peace of mind. Jade is said to give the user luck, friendship, and success. Jade is used to enhance dreams to unlock hidden knowledge and connect to your higher self, while also keeping you from harm. | the immune system, cleansing toxins from the organs and blood, healing stitches, supporting kidney function, promoting fertility and aiding childbirth, relieving menstrual pain and symptoms. |  |
|---|---|---|---|
| Hematite | Energizing Hematite is a protective crystal | Helping circulatory problems, | Root |

| | | | |
|---|---|---|---|
| | that will energize, ground, and vitalize the body. It encourages optimism, courage, self-discipline, and self-improvement. Hematite has the ability to harmonize the mind, body, and soul and disperse negative energy. | increasing oxygen in the blood, stimulating the spleen, liver, and gallbladder, reducing stress and muscle cramps. | |
| Polychronic Jasper | Stability Polychronic jasper is also referred to as desert jasper. It symbolizes the earth, and is therefore a grounding stone that gives you stability and balance in all areas of your life. | Supporting the digestive system and circulatory system, stimulating the function of sexual organs. | Root, Sacral, & Solar Plexus |

| | | | |
|---|---|---|---|
| | It also brings balance to vibrations and emotional energies in your body, such as assertiveness and sensitivity. | | |
| Labradorite | Spiritual Connection Labradorite is a protective crystal that is often used in meditation to direct energies with higher intensity so that you can connect to your true self and realize your ultimate spiritual purpose. Labradorite also clears and protects your aura from outside influences, strengthens | Balancing hormones, lowering blood pressure, aiding eye and brain disorders, and treating the common cold. | Heart, Third-Eye, & Crown |

| | intuition, and raises your consciousness. | | |
|---|---|---|---|
| Lemurian Seeded | Wisdom Leumarian seeded is believed to have been used in the ancient civilization of Leumaria. The crystals are said to hold the wisdom and knowledge from the past, to bring an awakening to your spirit. Leumarian seeded promotes unconditional love, and the ability to move past the boundaries we've set for ourselves to ignite our spirit and help us reach our full potential. | Healing diseases, opening energy channels in the spiritual and physical bodies. | All Chakras |

| | | | |
|---|---|---|---|
| | These crystals are also exceptional healers and are often used for balancing the chakras. | | |
| Moonstone | New Beginnings This stone has the power to bring about new beginnings. It has a strong connection to the moon, and brings a calming and uplifting energy to whoever uses it. Moonstone is also used to help strengthen intuition and female energy, as well as promote psychic abilities. | Calming emotions, relieving anxiety and stress, alleviating menstrual pains and symptoms, and promoting digestive and reproductive health. | Sacral & Heart |
| Moss Agate | Courage & Strength Moss agate promotes | Strengthening muscles, relieving emotional | Heart |

| | | | |
|---|---|---|---|
| | strength, courage, stability, and grounding. Agate is the crystal of acceptance, helping those who use it find their truth. It eliminates negative energy and brings peace of mind. | tension, promoting healthy digestive system, and treating skin disorders. | |
| Nuummite | The Sorcerer's Stone No, you didn't read that wrong; nuummite is also known as the "sorcerer's stone." It draws on power from fiery energies from the earth and from that, it gives you inner power and unparallelled clairvoyance. It gives you good | Healing the energy of the user, and directing healing energy onto others. | All Chakras |

| | | | |
|---|---|---|---|
| | fortune, protection, and courage. Nuummite also has the unique ability to relieve those who are stuck in their subconscious fear and past trauma. | | |
| Peridot | Compassion Peridot promotes compassion, positive energy, and encourages spiritual rebirth. This stone also brings prosperity and harmony to relationships. | Reducing stress and negative feelings such as jealousy and anger, healing ulcers, and aiding digestive issues. | Heart |
| Petrified Wood | Harmony Petrified wood encourages inner harmony to help you see the positive side of life. Petrified wood will relieve | Treating arthritis, aiding rheumatism and blood clots, strengthening the skeletal system and muscle tissue, | Root, Sacral, & Solar Plexus |

| | | | |
|---|---|---|---|
| | any worry or stress you're carrying. It will also give you composure to allow you to accept whatever challenges come your way. | calming nerves, and improving appetite. | |
| Pyrite Cube | Protection Pyrite is known as the crystal of protection. It repels negative energy and physical danger. Pyrite simulates intellect and encourages good health, emotional strength, and positivity. | Relieving anxiety and negative emotions, improving digestion and circulation, and promoting healthy brain function. | Root, Solar Plexus, & Heart |
| Red Aventurine | Possibility & Opportunity Red aventurine increases creativity, the ability to identify | Improving circulation, healing nerves, and promoting reproductive health and | Root & Sacral |

| | | | |
|---|---|---|---|
| | possibilities, and prosperity. It also enhances the five senses. | immunity. | |
| Red Jasper | Grounding & Stimulating Red jasper symbolizes the earth, and is therefore a grounding stone that encourages overall stability and balance. It promotes courageous and vital energy. Red jasper radiates tranquility and gives you the peace and support to face your problems head on. | Improving circulation, promoting healthy digestive and circulatory systems, enhancing the function of sexual organs. | Root |
| Red Phantom Quartz | Healing Red phantom quartz draws its power from the | Recovering from addictions and compulsive behaviors, | Heart |

| | | | |
|---|---|---|---|
| | earth to promote healing of past trauma and pain. This crystal is also great for stimulating inspiration, intellect, and intuition. | treating inflammation, anemia, and circulatory issues. | |
| Rhodonite | Emotional Balance Rhodonite brings emotional balance, nurturing, and love. It encourages a clear heart, grounding energy, and helps the user realize and achieve their greatest potential. It also heals emotional pain and self-doubt. | Treating insect bites, reducing the appearance of scars, aiding bone development, healing organs, stimulating fertility, and treating auto-immune diseases and stomach ulcers. | Heart |

| | | | |
|---|---|---|---|
| Rose Quartz | Peace & Love Rose quartz encourages unconditional love, peace, compassion, and forgiveness. It brings harmony and balance to relationships and relieves stress to allow us to openly express love and empathy towards ourselves and others. This lovely crystal promotes inner healing, trust, and self-worth. It is the crystal of universal love and can be used to attract love into your life and promote healthy relationships. | Strengthening the heart and circulatory systems, detoxing impurities, promoting fertility, and aiding the healing of respiratory ailments. | Heart |

| | | | |
|---|---|---|---|
| Septarian | Communication Septarian has the power to enhance communication abilities and heal relationships. It is an uplifting stone that helps the user better understand themselves on a spiritual level. This unique stone allows you to face the challenges of everyday life with grace and confidence. | Relieving pain, boosting the immune system, relieving cramps and muscle spasms, and treating benign growths. | Heart, Throat, & Third-Eye |
| Shungite | The Wonder Stone This particular stone also goes by another name, "the wonder stone." This stone is estimated to be over two billion years old. It | Clearing negative energies, treating dysfunctional behaviors, and neutralizing harmful organisms in your body. | All Chakras |

| | | | |
|---|---|---|---|
| | radiates positivity and good fortune. Shungite has the power to absorb negative energies and transform them into positive energies. It also aids in psychic development and protection. | | |
| Shiva Lingam | Unified Male and Female Energies Shiva Lingam are sacred stones of the Hindu religion. It intensifies the vitality of your life force. Only found in India, shiva lingam activate the slumbering kundalini. It is representative of sexuality and unifying the male and female | Promoting the electrical current of the body's systems, treating infertility, and relieving menstrual pains and symptoms. | Root & Sacral |

| | | | |
|---|---|---|---|
| | energies. | | |
| Smoky Quartz | Clearing Energy<br>Smoky quartz dispels negative energy and blocked chakras. It is sedative, grounding, and centering. Smoky quartz is used to enhance awareness and recollect important dreams. | Aiding the treatment of depression, detoxing the body of impurities, relieving stress and anxiety, neutralizing radiation, and improving the digestive system. | Root |
| Sodalite | Truth<br>Sodalite promotes intelligence, intuition, clarity, truth, and perception. It brings calmness, rational thought, emotional balance, and | Relieving insomnia, improving the immune system, dispelling radiation, treating throat and larynx ailments, lowering fevers | Throat & Third-Eye |

|  | confidence. This stone is primarily used to build trust and faith in yourself, so that you can stand up for your beliefs and dispel fears that hold you back from accepting your path. | and blood pressure, and boosting the metabolism. |  |
|---|---|---|---|
| Spirit Quartz | Uplifting Although it is a relatively young crystal, spirit quartz has powerful properties. It promotes spiritual alignment and introspection. Spirit quartz is used to bring clarity when you're faced with challenges. This | Overcoming trauma and grief, healing skin damage, melanoma, and skin allergies, and overcoming addictions. | All Chakras; using the Crown to connect with the entire chakra system. |

| | | | |
|---|---|---|---|
| | crystal holds the vibration of universal love and rebirth, aligning the chakras, and bringing balance to male and female energies. | | |
| Tibetan Quartz | Protection Tibetan quartz can be found in the Himalayas of Tibet, which is regarded as one of the most sacred places on earth. Tibetan quartz radiates light and positive energy, which will transfer to your aura and protect it. The crystal purifies negative influences and brings balance to all the chakras. | Healing the nervous system, treating dysfunctional behaviors, and protecting against negative electromagnetic energies. | All Chakras |

| | | | |
|---|---|---|---|
| Tiger's Eye | Power and Strength As the name suggests, tiger's eye will bring you courage, strength, confidence, and good fortune. This stone has the power to sharpen your senses, enhance intuition, and ground you in your beliefs. It also brings clarity, self-empowerment, and good judgement. | Relieving headaches, treating digestive disorders, aiding the spleen, pancreas, and colon, improving reproductive health, and alleviating asthma attacks. | Sacral & Solar Plexus |
| Tiger Iron | Manifestation & Strength Tiger iron is a combination of hematite, tiger's eye, and red jasper; therefore, it holds many of the same | Improving physical energy and strength, improving circulation, increasing red and white blood cell count, boosting the | Root, Sacral, & Solar Plexus |

| | | | |
|---|---|---|---|
| | properties of it's parent stones. This particular stone inspires creativity and brings balance into your life when faced with difficult situations. It is also a good stone for manifesting your desired outcome in times of trouble. Tiger iron is a grounding stone that will bring you strength and vitality. | immune system, and improving the function of the nervous system. | |
| Black Tourmaline | Support Black tourmaline is a supportive stone that will bring protection from negative external forces, stress, and | Restoring healthy sleeping patterns, strengthening the immune system, relieving pain, improving the function of | Root |

| | | | |
|---|---|---|---|
| | negative energy. It is a grounding stone that will anchor your positive spirit, promote wisdom, individuality, patience, and inner peace. | the adrenal glands, colon, and spine movement. | |
| Tourmalated Quartz | Empowerment & Protection Tourmalated quartz promotes light in your aura, and healing on the physical, emotional, and spiritual levels. This crystal will give you a sense of spiritual grounding, as well as psychic protection. | Regenerating the nervous system and relieving stress and depression. | Root |
| Zebra Marble | Transformation Zebra marble helps in self-development, | Aiding the treatment of allergies, improving the | Solar Plexus |

| | transformation, and liberation in overcoming inner struggles and unhappiness. It will open your eyes and mind to new perspectives and brainstorming creative solutions to difficult problems. | function of the kidneys, spleen, and intestines, restoring muscle tissue, and improving skin disorders. | |
|---|---|---|---|

# CHAPTER 4: CARING FOR YOUR CRYSTALS & OTHER USES

Healing crystals have become increasingly popular among spiritual enthusiasts and social media personalities. If you haven't yet found yourself completely decided on the practice, finding the right place to buy your crystals can be overwhelming and even stressful. This is especially true if you're like me and want to buy crystals that are comforting and have meaning.

As someone who struggled with self- confidence growing up, and wanting to find acceptance and my inner truth, I only trusted one place when shopping for my crystals; the local metaphysical store.

Today, you can easily buy crystals from online retailers. The problem is that the collection of online stores all list hundreds of stone varieties that you can buy, but without actually listing the descriptions of the crystals' properties. For someone who is new to crystal practices, it can be intimidating when choosing the right stone.

On the other side of the coin, there are plenty of websites that genuinely serve and inform their customers. Afterall, crystal users are an authentic community that simply want to help others achieve self- actualization. These types of websites will typically feature carefully curated collections, customizable stone sets, and founders who are truly knowledgeable backing them.

# The In's and Out's of Buying Crystals Online

The truth of the matter is that there is no one place to buy crystals, both online and in real life. You can get quality genuine crystals from local shops and online. However, faux crystals are something that newcomers and experts alike need to stay aware of.

But don't let this keep you from exploring the practice of crystal healing or any other new age traditions. Imitation crystals are to be expected, just like in any other industry. Hey, fake money and fake fur exist, you can't expect any business not to have counterfeits wandering around out there.

One of the greatest benefits of buying crystals from a conventional shop is that you can inspect the crystals up close and from all angles; plus the added bonus of seeing if you have a physical reaction to the stone. It makes picking out tumble stones and small crystal points that much easier.

However, the internet has allowed crystal users to purchase crystals that they would never otherwise have access to a decade ago. If you don't buy crystals from online vendors, then you may never get your hands on the stones that you really want; unless you live near a mine.

There are many pros and cons to buying crystals both online and in- person. There is no "best" way to purchase a crystal, so I put together a list of tips that will help guide you through the process. One of the biggest downsides to buying crystals online is that you don't get to hold the crystal before purchasing it. Just going off of an image, you don't get to experience the true color, size, or energy before getting it delivered.

# Tip #1: Always buy from a well-known, reputable vendor.

This may sound obvious, but in a time when anyone with a credit card can buy a website and accept money online, caution needs to be practiced. Look at the seller's reviews, scrutinize the pictures of crystals that they post, and ask questions when you can. Many online retailers have social media pages and contact information; use that to your advantage and ask questions about where they source their crystals and their energetic properties.

# Tip #2: Use your own research to guide your way.

You can also use this book or other gem guides to help you identify authentic stones. Of course, some of this knowledge will simply come with experience. If a cheap crystal seems too good to be true, then there's a good chance it isn't the real thing. Although many websites will list a crystal's properties, it's best to go off of your own research and understanding to guide your purchasing. A lot of sellers out there will overly hype up the stone's powers and give out false information to make a sale. While it's not uncommon to mistake a crystal's energetic properties, if a retailer continuously posts inaccurate information, they are probably not the company you should be buying from.

## Tip #3: Always, always check the price!

Oh, my friend, I cannot emphasize this enough. I know it may sound like common sense, but even I have made this mistake more than once. Always check to see where you are purchasing your crystals from and how much the shipping price is. I've mistakenly bought crystals from a vendor in Turkey, and continued with the purchase without double-checking the shipping information.

The end result was me paying more money that I would've liked to on the crystal, and also waiting two weeks for it to arrive in the mail. Granted, the crystal I was searching for was more rare, so I still probably would've bought it. But, the shipping information will also come into play if you're buying from overseas vendors who don't know your country's customs laws.

## Tip #4: Be aware of the red flags and steer clear from questionable merchants.

1. I have six rules of thumb that I follow when buying from an online vendor; and I pass them onto you in hopes that you won't make the same mistakes I did. The red flags to watch out for are as follows:

2. They don't respond to emails at all, or take more than three days to reply to an email.

3. The vendor doesn't have an active social media presence or has been inactive on their profile for more than six months.

4. The photos of their products are dark or blurry.

5. You get an "out of stock email" after ordering a product.

6. They have a small selection of crystals to choose from.

7. Your packages are delivered badly wrapped.

# Caring for Your Crystals: Cleansing and Recharging

The first thing you should do when receiving a crystal is to cleanse it. Crystals have the ability to naturally absorb whatever energy it meets on its path. Cleansing the stone removes any negative energy it may have picked up along its journey to you.

Likewise, it is also important to cleanse crystals after you have been working with them, especially in energetically-charged practices such as meditation or chakra rebalancing. This is because they will also absorb the person's energy that you have been working with, and the energy the stone took in could be passed on to someone else if it is not cleaned out.

You may be wondering how you will know if and when a crystal needs to be cleansed. The best answer I can give you is, with practice and experience, you will intuitively know when a crystal needs to be cleansed. For instance, quartz crystal will become cloudy appearance, when they are typically bright and clear. Other stones will lack their soft glow. Believe it or not, some crystals will even physically feel heavier or more dense, because of all the energy they are holding.

Any crystals that you wear or space around the house will have to be cleansed on a regular basis. Of course how often you cleanse them will depend on how often you wear the crystal or how much activity is going on inside the house. Once again, you own instinct is your best guide. If a stone is just not giving you the same feeling as it did before, then it's time to cleanse it. There are several ways to cleanse a crystal; with water, sage, moonlight, and sunlight.

## Water Cleansing

You can cleanse your crystal with water by holding it under clean running water or placing it in a clean glass that is filled with fresh water. You can also add pink himalayan salt for an added boost in clearing negative energies. If you happen to live near an ocean or clean stream, then it is best to wash your crystals there.

Natural bodies of water are always preferred to tap water. Remember that your intention plays a role in everything you do with crystals. So, as you're going through the process of clearing away the harmful energies, keep your intention in mind as you re-energize your crystal.

## Nature Cleansing

Every organic thing around you emits its own energy and vibrations. It is no coincidence that crystal healers also love filling their spaces with plants. Both offer radiating positive vibrations that can feed your soul. Crystals love plants, and you can magnify energy by putting your crystals near flourishing plants. In turn, this will benefit both the crystals and the plants.

## Sunlight & Moonlight Cleansing

Just like any other living organism, crystals love sunlight. The natural power and energy simply fills our being with joy and warmth, and crystals react no differently that we do when placed in direct sunlight! If you are lacking in the vegetation department and don't live near the ocean, you can open the blinds and put your crystals on the windowsill and get the same result.

Make sure that you choose a window that receives direct sunlight during the day. On the other hand, if you are feeling bold adventuresome, you can try burying crystals in soil in a secure place overnight. It is always best to do this during a full moon, as that is when the crystal will collect the most energy. Just like the beaming sun, luminous moonlight will also recharge your crystals.

## Sage or Sweetgrass Cleansing

With this next cleansing method, I offer a friendly word of caution not to burn yourself while getting the sage to start burning. Smudging with sage is a well-known, if not common, practice. You can burn either sage or sweetgrass in a heat- safe dish, and carefully pass your crystal through the smoke. Once again, repeat your intention and envision the outcome as you do this.

## Sound Cleansing

Sound cleansing is another new age practice that is slowly making its way into the mainstream. Not that I'm one for pop culture, but even celebrities like the Kardashians, Robert

Downey Jr, and Charlize Theron are huge advocates for sound baths. Sound bathing is when you allow a single continuous pitch or tone to wash over the crystal.

You can do this with chanting, bells, or singing bowls. It doesn't matter what key you use or how you make the sound, as long as the sound itself is loud enough to encompass the stone. You can sound bathe multiple crystals at the same time, which is handy when your collection really starts to grow. Sound cleansing should take approximately five to ten minutes.

## Recharging Crystals

You can also recharge crystals to renew their energy. Now, there is a difference between cleansing and charging a crystal. Not all cleansing methods will charge your crystal, and vice versa. For example, smudging with sage will bind and dispel negative energy, but it won't energize your crystal. The only method that will effectively do both is sunlight. You can recharge a crystal by:

Placing the crystal in direct sunlight for about one hour. You'll know when the crystal is finished charging when it physically appears to be brighter and feels lighter in your hand. Sunlight will charge most crystals efficiently, but you can also use the light of the moon and stars and achieve a similar result.

Using sound waves. You just learned how to cleanse a crystal with sound, and you can also recharge it. However, in order to add a vibration frequency to a crystal, the sound you use must be of a higher frequency than the inherent vibration of the crystal. You'll be able to tell when you've found the right frequency when the crystal shows more luster.

Placing the crystal in dynamic weather conditions. For example, putting your crystal outside during a thunderstorm will provide an electromagnetic charge. Plus, you can kill two birds with one stone and cleanse the crystal in the moonlight, leaving it outside buried under soil overnight.

Using an amethyst cluster or clear quartz cluster. You can charge other stones by placing them on amethyst or quartz clusters that have been programmed to re- energize other crystals.

## Safely Storing Crystals

Crystals love to be placed in open spaces because it allows them to work to their full potential. But, if you like to carry stones with you throughout the day, then you should store them in small bags made of silk, cotton, satin, or velvet; basically any bag that isn't created from a man-made fabrics. Crystals should be treated carefully. They may be powerful specimens, but they can still chip or split. I've learned the hard way just how important proper storage is when it comes to caring for your crystals. Let's just say, I've managed to pick up a few helpful tips and tricks along the way.

- Keep them in a dry and clean location. Any exposure to humidity, excess moisture, dust, or even salty air (like outside near the ocean), can cause damage to the stones.

- For unique and expensive crystals that are hard to come by, they should be stored in plastic containers or acid- free boxes.

- For softer, more fragile crystals, they should be kept in individual containers that are lined with fabric or tissue to keep from being damaged. An eco- friendly way to store small crystals is in an egg carton or wooden jewelry box.

- It's best to separate your crystals when storing them. You can do this any number of ways: by color, chakra, tumble stones, raw stones, value, healing properties, and size are just a few examples. There's really no "right" or "wrong" way to store crystals - do whatever feels right for you!

- Don't ever use cotton balls or cotton padding to line your boxes, because the fibers can stick to stones with ragged edges. However, it's perfectly fine to do when storing tumbled stones.

## Other Ways to Use Crystal Healing

When it comes to crystal healing, each stone is unique and is not easily replaced. I've spent over a decade collecting crystals from all over the world, each of them are special to me and have their own story. Every one of my crystals were collected at a single point in time, and each hold a unique geologic history. They are treasures from the earth and should be treated with respect and care.

### Tools

If you are just beginning your crystal healing journey, it may be difficult to understand just how and why these stones work. Crystals are tools for manifesting your intentions to create the life you want. They connect us to the earth because they are physical, palpable specimens that have powerful vibrations. Their energy will keep you connected to your intentions just by holding them close to your skin or keeping them in your home. Every thought, intention, and vibration is captured and them amplified through the crystals to bring your goals and dreams into manifestation.

Crystal healing is deeply rooted in our history. Clear quartz has been on this planet since the beginning of time. It has been valued in ancient civilizations, used as protective talismans, peace offerings, and adornments. In fact, quartz makes up approximately twelve percent of the planet's crust today.

It's also used in almost every piece of technology that we use on a daily basis. If it is possible for crystals to use their powers to communicate through computer chips and telecommunication technology, then it doesn't seem so silly for a crystal's inherent vibrational energy to transform other things too. But, more on this in the next chapter!

## Programming

Before you can use a crystal, you have to program it. This is possibly the most overlooked components in crystal healing. Basically, you have to give your crystal a purpose by programming it, or setting your intention. You have to tell crystals what to do if you want it to work for you.

When you find yourself in low moments, when you're doubting yourself and are vibrating at a lower frequency, your intentions and goals can seem impossible. Reconnecting with a programmed crystal will remind you of your limitless potential and give you the drive to push forward with renewed confidence.

Programming a crystal is a simple task. The first thing you need to do is cleanse the crystal, using whatever method resonates with you the most. After you've cleansed the crystal, hold it in your hands, close your eyes, and breathe deeply. Meditate on your faith, the things and people that make you happy, and how you want your life to change for the better.

While in this state of love and warmth, ask the universe, God, or whatever your highest vibration may be, to clear all unwanted energy from your crystal. Finally, either out loud or to yourself, command that the crystal holds the intention of "...," and then say what your intention is. Repeat this intention at least three times. End the programming session by saying "thank you" three times; to emphasize that your intention is already existent within the universe.

Once a crystal has been programmed, it will emit the energetic vibration of your vocalized intention until it is cleansed once again. You can cleanse and program your crystals as many times as you would like; they will always be there for you in any situation, big or small.

# Other Ways to Use Your Crystals

## Wear your crystals.

The more you make physical contact with your crystals, the more you can sue their energy. Therefore, wearing your crystals is one of the best strategies in making your intentions manifest. You can find crystals in literally every type of jewelry, and even in beauty products.

## Put them in your pocket, purse, or backpack.

If wearing your crystals as jewelry isn't your style, you can always carry your stones in a bag or pocket. Keeping your crystal in a place where you can easily touch it will help keep you grounded throughout the day.

## Use your crystals in meditation.

I know that meditation sounds like an over-hyped practice, but it really does work; especially in an age when over stimulation is a constant drain on our energy. To increase your daily dose of spiritual energy, hold your crystals while you are meditating to connect with their transcending powers. Keep in mind that you aren't praying to the crystal. You are holding them as a tool to get more connected to your higher self.

## Create a crystal layout on your body before starting the day.

It would be a lie to say none of us need an extra boost of energy in the morning. Let's be honest, a cup of coffee can only go so far. To mentally and spiritually prepare yourself for the day ahead, lay down and put a few crystals on your body. Focus on your breath as you steep in the high vibrations of the stones. Even just five minutes of laying with your crystals will create a tangible shift in your energy.

## Add them to your bath.

Unfortunately, it's not very often that you get to have a relaxing spa- inspired bath. But, when you've finally found the time, the best way to elevate your bath time experience is by placing crystals in your tub. Now, not every crystal is meant to be submerged in water; so double- check if it's okay before putting them in water.

## Add them to your ritual.

If you are looking for transformative, deep healing, then a crystal ritual may the the answer. If you are ready and willing to heal emotional wounds, let go of past traumatic experiences, or let go of limiting beliefs, then you can hold a crystal over your heart for fifteen to thirty minutes, and allow the energy to change you.

## Precautions

I know that it can be exciting to start using crystals, especially when you begin experiencing their power first-hand. However, it is crucial not to use too many healing crystals at once. This is because having so many crystals, all with different purposes and intentions, can result in a lack of focus.

It's like overflowing your plate at a buffet; putting more food than you can eat on your plate will inevitably lead to spoilage or retching. This concept remains true with the inherent rules of nature. Excess will result in regress. Balance is the natural order of nature. A lack of balance will ultimately lead to chaos.

Crystals are the fruit of mother nature, the very essence of the earth. Therefore, using too many crystals all at the same time will be counter- intuitive. But another reason not to use an overabundance of crystals is because it will result in a lack of focus for you, the user. Healing with crystals is heavily implanted in meditative practices - giving all of your attention to one purpose, one intention to make it come true.

Humans, especially today, already lack focus because of the constant stimulation from technology, fears of missing out on experiences or things, and being exposed to so many temptations and distractions. For a healing crystal's power to work, you need to meditate in tranquility and silence.

Your energy will go wherever your intention directs it. If your intentions are all over the place, how do you expect the crystals to work? Keep your mind clutter- free and stay focused and motivated on the most important goals. You can always cleanse and re-program your crystals later.

# CHAPTER 5: THE OTHER SIDE OF CRYSTAL HEALING

My friend, as we reach the end of our journey together, I would like to share with you one last personal story of mine. Now, I began this section with a warning. Because I believe that as an author, there is a responsibility I must take in making sure that whoever reads this guide is steered in the right path.

For me, crystal healing has absolutely changed my life. And while I will always continue practicing this art in its purest form, I will never tell you to ignore a medical professional's advice or avert you from conducting your own research.

I am a survivor of many things. I have experienced trauma, tragedy, loss, depression, and a medical diagnosis that was on track to end in the worst way. In the face of all this adversity, I held strong to my beliefs, my faith. Surrounded by naysayers, non- believers, and online articles and studies that told me I was crazy to put my life in a practice that has no scientific proof to back it up, I never wavered in my practice.

Because I had experienced firsthand the personal healing that crystals and new age practices had given me. I guarantee that if you go onto an online search engine right now and type in "crystal healing," you will find at least a dozen articles about how the practice is all a bunch of made up hooey, just on the first two pages of results.

My advice to you is that whether you are dealing with emotional damage, physical trauma, or any kind of suffering, you should listen to your doctors but also hold strong in your "new age" beliefs. I will never say that crystal healing doesn't work, or that it won't work for you, because my own experience proves otherwise.

But, if you are following your doctor's orders, continuing whatever treatment, or are just looking for something new and different to try to give you hope, then why not try crystal healing? What is the worst thing that could happen? You think it doesn't work and close that chapter in your life and move on. Or, you always wonder whether or not it would have made any difference.

This last chapter is for the naysayers, and anyone who is doubting giving crystal healing a try. It is also a caution for you, so that you understand crystal healing on all fronts. Personally, I believe that information is the greatest tool one can use. And to fully understand a practice or belief system, one must be aware of all the information out there, not just what serves their purpose.

Over the last few years, alternative wellness practices, like salt therapy lights and yoga classes have officially made their way into the mainstream. Crystal healing as a form of therapy and self- care has increasingly gained popularity, popping up all over social media, YouTube, yoga studios, and even on your coworker's desk.

In fact, consumers in the United States spend approximately thirty billion dollars every year on alternative and holistic medicine. However, despite the fact that crystal use has seen a surge of acclaim and demand recently, this practice is not favored or recognized by most medical practitioners and scientists. In fact, many of them refer to crystal use as a pseudoscience.

On a scientific level, there is a lack of evidence showing the crystal healing can be used to treat diseases or ailments. This is primarily because the diseases we face today have not been proven to be the product of an energy flow in our physical being. Websites and bloggers that promote crystal healing trace the tradition back at least six thousand years, to the ancient Sumerians of Mesopotamia, the ancient Egyptians, and the Mayans.

However, the modern philosophy of crystal treatment is not based on the beliefs of those civilizations; which primarily used crystals in adornments to ward off illness and negative vibrations. Instead, the concepts which are widely accepted and practiced now are based on traditions from Asian cultures. This is most notable in the Chinese concept of chi, or life energy, as well as the Hindu and Buddhist theories of chakras, which connects the physical body to the supernatural parts.

Although there are no scientific investigations on the effectiveness of crystal healing, there is a recent study that has suggested a placebo effect to be reasoning behind the practice's success. Placebo effects are the results that follow a treatment that are not directly linked to the treatment attempt itself affecting the disease of the patient. Basically, an individual might feel better after attending a crystal healing treatment, but there is no solid evidence that the result will correlate at all with the crystals being used during treatment.

This is the number one argument that non- believers will use to dispute the effectiveness of crystal healing. However, brain imaging studies have actually shown that when a patient takes a sugar pill or gets a mock acupuncture treatment, it activates specific regions in the brain that can positively affect the patient by releasing hormones like dopamine and endorphins; which are your body's natural pain killers.

This is a real biological process, not just something crystal users are lying about for their own device. There have been a number of studies that have shown when patients are given a drug and told that it will relieve their pain, they will respond twice as well as when they are given that drug unknowingly. This actually suggests that effectiveness of many prescription drugs on the market really comes from the power of expectation.

There is a statistic that says eighty percent of dietary supplement users would keep taking their supplements, even if medical or government officials say that it would not be effective. I believe that time and time again personal experience trumps anything that science will claim. I know that not everyone will share this belief or ideology, but it would be ignorant to ignore or disregard someone's actual experience just because there's no scientific proof to show for it. For example, the fitness industry is filled with weight loss supplements, programs, and influencers who swear by one method or another. In many cases, one size does not fit all.

What worked really well for one person will not always work the same for the next. It's like comparing the ketogenic diet to intuitive eating- both may work for some people, but there will ultimately be people who have completely different experiences. As long as people are reaching their goals and getting the results they want, who cares what program they are following to do it as long as it's safe?

One of the very first pieces of scientific evidence that showed the power of crystals was by spiritual scientist Marcel Vogel of the IBM San Jose Research Center. Working with crystals for twenty- seven years, Vogel watched crystals grow under a microscope. And he noted that their shape grew into whatever form he was thinking about.

Vogel's hypothesis was that the vibrations were the reaction to the continuous assembling and disassembling of bonds between the molecules. He also conducted tests to show the supernatural power in quartz to prove the rocks can store thoughts in the same manner that tapes use magnetic energy to capture sound. Even Albert Einstein believed that everything in life is vibration. He believed that your intentions matched the vibrations and energy of everything that manifested before you.

Every single day, we have the ability to choose our thoughts as we go through our journey. We have infinite opportunities and unlimited energy to consume and put out into the world. With every new beginning and new challenge, healing crystals are a reminder that we can connect to the universe and use the healing vibrations of the earth to create the lives we want and deserve.

The most important lesson to take away from crystal healing is patience. Because just like the thousands of years it took for those crystals and semi- precious stones to develop and evolve, working with crystals will also take time.

As you learn and progress through this journey, use your crystals as a reminder to practice gratitude for the abundance of opportunity and mystery given to you by the universe.

# Conclusion

M y dear friend, thank you so much for following me through this journey. One year ago, I set out to write down my own experience with crystal healing so that I can pass my knowledge onto anyone who was curious about using crystals and wanted to start down their own path of enlightenment.

I know that it can be hard to invest yourself into something that you're afraid won't payout in the end. But I have every ounce of faith that you will continue forward with more confidence and grace than before.

It is truly amazing how Mother Nature provides us with everything we could possibly need to not just live, but enjoy this life. We are all part of the same working, living, breathing organism; trying to find our own way while withstanding adversity and hardship.

Please believe me when I say that no one has to go through this adventure alone, and I am so grateful to have been a part of your experience. If our paths never meet again, I wish you only the best moving forward. I hope that I was able to show you just how powerful energy can be, when you put purpose and intention behind it.

Afterall, the crystals will never work if you don't work to put your own positive energy out there into the universe. Continue giving unconditionally, and continue down your path of healing and exploring. It's a road not taken often enough, especially during a time of overwhelming negativity. Always remember that you have the power to make this life whatever you want it to be.

Lastly, thank you for reading this book. The opportunity to make a positive impact on another person's life and to be an example of all that crystal healing can do is truly wonderful. I wish you the very best.

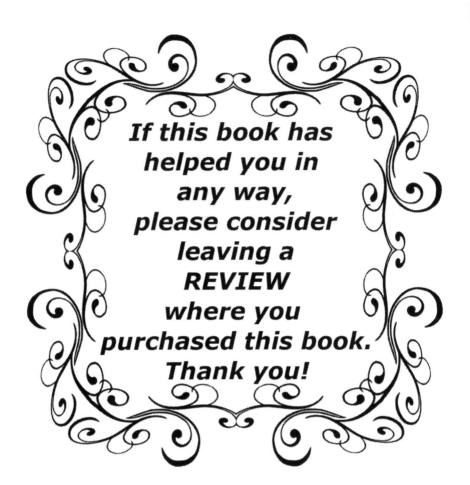

If this book has helped you in any way, please consider leaving a REVIEW where you purchased this book. Thank you!

Printed in Great Britain
by Amazon

38381210R00077